CALLING ALL KIDS

Hey Kids! Are you looking for some really AWESOME sewing projects? Check out this leaflet and discover why QUILTING is all the rage!

These **7 projects**, designed with YOU in mind are **FAST, FUN, and TOTALLY COOL.** With our easy instructions, your choice of fabrics and a little help from an adult, you will be quilting in no time!

Choose from a fold-up **sewing caddy** — just the thing for storing your small sewing supplies, a really cool **tote bag** that's as much fun to make as it is to carry, a **throw quilt** that you can make in YOUR favorite colors — perfect for jazzing up your room, a **photo transfer pillow** made for showing off your favorite pictures, a huge **floor pillow** — great for lounging while watching TV or visiting with friends, and much more! These are definitely NOT your Grandma's quilts!

"Sew" pick out your project, gather your tools, your fabrics, and an adult and get ready to learn to **QUILT!**

LEISURE ARTS, INC.
Little Rock, Arkansas

D1398490

NOTE FOR PARENTS AND TEACHERS

We have designed this book to help you teach kids ages 8-14, who have had some experience sewing by hand and machine, how to **machine piece** and to **quilt**. It is not intended to teach basic sewing skills such as hand sewing, threading and using a sewing machine, or pressing with an iron.

Because your child may be using a rotary cutter, **safety** is our first concern. Although we have included instructions on how to safely use this tool, we recommend adult supervision at all times when your child is rotary cutting. If your child is under the age of ten, you may want them to use scissors for all cutting or you may wish to precut the fabric pieces for your child.

Teaching a child to quilt provides quality one-on-one time with your child and establishes a link between learning and fun. Quilting promotes their creativity, helps to develop their reading and comprehension skills, and gives them a sense of pride and accomplishment. To further support your child:

- Encourage them to choose fabrics, buttons, ribbons, and other project supplies in colors and prints that appeal to them. You will be amazed at just how artistic a child can be.
- Read and become familiar with the **Things You Need To Know** and **General Instructions** sections. Be prepared to answer questions during the lessons.
- Be aware of your child's skill level and help them choose a project appropriate for them. The projects are presented in order from easiest to most complicated. Some children may need to start with Lesson 1, where as others may be able to begin with a more complex project.

We hope that you and your child have a pleasurable experience working together on these projects and that your child develops a lifelong love of quilting.

THINGS YOU NEED TO KNOW

The entire process of making a quilt is called **quilting**.

The two tightly woven edges of fabric are called the **selvages**. Some selvages are a different color from the fabric and have information about the manufacturer printed on them.

The direction of the threads in woven fabric is called the **grain.** The direction from selvage to selvage is called the **crosswise grain** and the direction that is parallel to the selvage is called the **lengthwise grain**. The diagonal (from corner to corner) of fabric is called the **bias**.

Sewing shapes cut from fabric (such as hearts) onto a larger background piece of fabric by hand or machine is called **appliqué**.

Sewing shapes such as squares, rectangles, or triangles together by hand or machine is called **piecing**.

The distance between the seam (the stitches) and the cut edge of the fabric is called the **seam allowance**. In quilting, the seam allowance is usually ¼".

A **block** is a fabric shape that is pieced, appliquéd or cut from a single fabric and is usually square. Blocks are sewn together to make a **quilt top**.

Units are two or more fabric shapes that are sewn together to make a part of a block. Two or more units are then sewn together to make a block.

Setting Squares are cut from a single fabric and are the same size as your pieced or appliquéd blocks. They are placed between the blocks in a quilt top.

Sashings are the rectangular strips sewn between blocks. They are usually cut from a contrasting fabric to frame the blocks.

The long rectangular strips sewn around the outer edges of a quilt top are called **borders**. Borders can be pieced or cut from a single fabric.

A quilt is made of 3 layers like a sandwich; the **quilt top** (the pretty part on top), the **batting** (the fluffy middle layer), and the **backing** (the bottom layer). The **quilting** (the decorative stitches) holds the layers together.

Batting is made from cotton, polyester, wool, silk, or a blend of these materials. The thickness of batting (low, medium, or high) is called the **loft**.

The fabric strip that goes around the outside edges of a quilt is called the **binding**. The act of sewing that strip to the quilt is called **binding a quilt**.

3

GENERAL INSTRUCTIONS

Before you begin working on your project, take some time to read the General Instructions, pages 4-17, and study the photos and diagrams so you can learn about the techniques you will be using.

WHAT YOU NEED

Some of these basic supplies you will have at home already, the rest can easily be found in your local fabric or quilting stores. The instructions for each project **only** list the specific fabrics, buttons, ribbon, and other supplies needed for **that** project.

BASIC SUPPLIES

Scissors – One very sharp pair to use for cutting fabric and another for cutting paper or template plastic.

Fabric Marking Pencil – Used for tracing around templates or marking quilting lines on fabric. Choose one that shows up clearly on your fabric and can be easily removed.

Hand Quilting Needles – Size 5 or 6 crewel or embroidery needles.

Iron and Ironing Board – A household steam iron will be fine.

Quilting Hoop – (optional) Used to hold your project while you are hand quilting. Some quilters prefer to stitch without a hoop.

Sewing Machine – Any sewing machine that produces an even, straight stitch. Use size 80/12 universal (sharp-pointed) machine needles.

Straight Pins – Long, sharp, thin pins with round glass heads. Pins with flower-shaped heads are easy to see and to hold.

Thimble – A metal thimble with a flat top and deep dimples that fits snugly on the middle finger of your sewing hand.

Thread – General-purpose 100% cotton thread. Match your thread color to your fabric or use a neutral color such as a medium gray or tan.

SCISSOR CUTTING SUPPLIES

If you choose to cut with scissors, in addition to the **Basic Supplies** listed above, you will also need:

Fine-point Permanent Marker – To use for tracing patterns onto template plastic.

Template Plastic – Sheets of translucent plastic for making piecing or appliqué patterns (templates).

ROTARY CUTTING SUPPLIES

If you choose to cut with a rotary cutter, in addition to the **Basic Supplies** listed above, you will also need:

Rotary Cutter – An extremely sharp, round blade mounted on a plastic handle. For safety, look for one that the blade stays closed until you push down to cut (pressure sensitive).

Rotary Cutting Ruler – A thick clear acrylic ruler with $1/8$" crosswise and lengthwise markings. A 6" wide x 18" or 24" long is recommended.

Rotary Cutting Mat – A thick plastic mat with 1" grid lines designed to be used with a rotary cutter. An 18" x 24" or larger size is recommended.

Klutz Glove™ – (optional) Made from a unique heavy-duty cut-resistant material, it is worn on the hand holding the ruler to help protect you from injury when using a rotary cutter. (Remember, rotary cutters are extremely sharp!)

FABRICS

Follow the guidelines below to help you choose and prepare your fabrics.

CHOOSING THE RIGHT FABRICS

- Always use 100% cotton fabrics. Look for ones that feel smooth and are tightly woven with the threads close together (**Fig. 1**). Rough feeling fabric that is loosely woven and the threads are far apart is hard to work with and may stretch out of shape.

Fig. 1

- The fabric width is printed on the end of each bolt. In this leaflet, fabric requirements are based on 43/44" wide fabric. If you buy narrower fabric, you may not have enough. If you buy wider fabric you may have a lot left over.

- Pick fabrics in the colors YOU really like. Just because we show a project made with bright-colored fabrics doesn't mean it won't look equally as great if you use pastel or dark fabrics.

- For contrast, try using some light, medium, and dark shades of the colors you pick (**Fig. 2**).

Fig. 2

- To make your project even more interesting, use fabrics that have small, medium, and large prints (**Fig. 3**).

Fig. 3

- Repeating the same print in different colors, as we did in the **Pillow Topper**, page 36, looks great, too.

WASHING AND IRONING YOUR FABRICS

Washing and drying your fabrics before cutting keeps the dye in the darker fabrics from bleeding onto the lighter ones and pre-shrinks the fabric.

1. Unfold your fabric pieces and separate them into light and dark colors.
2. To help reduce raveling (threads coming loose along the cut edges), use scissors to snip a small triangle from each corner of your fabric pieces.
3. Machine-wash light and dark colors separately in warm water with a small amount of mild laundry detergent. Do not use fabric softener.
4. Dry your fabric pieces in the dryer, removing them while they are slightly damp.
5. Iron each piece until dry using a steam iron set on "Cotton."

TIP

To make tracing easier, you can tape the template plastic to the page with removable tape.

Making Templates

1. Lay a piece of template plastic over the pattern.
2. Using a fine-point permanent marker (and a ruler to help you trace over straight lines) carefully trace over the solid outer lines of the pattern onto the template plastic (**Fig. 4**).

Fig. 4

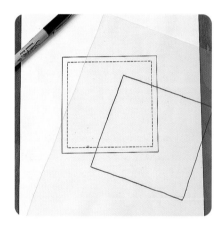

CUTTING

*Depending on your chosen cutting method, follow either **Scissor Cutting** or **Rotary Cutting**, page 8.*

SCISSOR CUTTING

CUTTING LARGE PIECES

Some project pieces such as large blocks, sashings, and borders, do not have patterns. Cutting instructions are given in measurements. Follow these steps to cut out these pieces.

1. Using the width of the selvage as a guide and keeping your cutting line straight, cut away the selvages from the length of your fabric.
2. Following the measurements given in the project's cutting instructions, use a ruler or yardstick and a fabric marking pencil to draw the shapes onto the wrong side of your fabric.
3. Cut out the shapes on the drawn lines.

MAKING AND USING TEMPLATES

Follow these steps to make and then use templates to cut out your fabric pieces.

3. Remove the tape, if used, and cut out the template on the drawn line (**Fig. 5**).

Fig. 5

TIP

Placing a sheet of extra-fine sandpaper under your fabric will help keep the fabric from slipping when drawing shapes or around templates.

4. Lay your template over the original pattern to be sure it is exactly the same size and shape as the pattern.

5. Repeat Steps 1-4 to make a template for each pattern in the project instructions.

Using Templates

1. Place the template face down on the wrong side of fabric (**Fig. 6**).

Fig. 6

2. To help you draw a smooth line, hold your fabric marking pencil at a slight angle to the fabric (**Fig. 7**).

Fig. 7

3. Drawing straight lines, which cross at the corners, is easier than trying to draw around the corners of a template (**Fig 8**).

Fig. 8

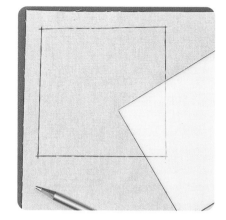

4. Draw around the template (**Fig. 9**). This will be your cutting line. Refer to **Fig. 10** if you need to use the template to draw the same shape multiple times on your fabric.

Fig. 9

Fig. 10

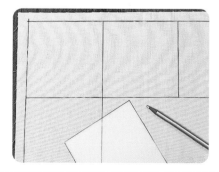

5. Cut out the fabric pieces **exactly** on the drawn line (**Fig. 11**).

Fig. 11

6. Repeat Steps 1-5 for each template in the project instructions.

CAUTION!

Always observe these safety precautions when using a rotary cutter, since it is extremely sharp:

- Cut in a direction **away** from your body.
- If your rotary cutter has a manual retractable blade, **immediately** close the blade after **each** cut.
- If your rotary cutter is pressure sensitive, **never** lock the blade in the open position.
- Wear shoes when using your rotary cutter to protect your feet and toes. A dropped rotary cutter can cause a very bad cut.
- Put your rotary cutter away in a **safe** place when you are finished using it.

ROTARY CUTTING

When rotary cutting, strips are always cut across the selvage-to-selvage width of the fabric unless your project instructions tell you to cut lengthwise strips.

SQUARING-UP THE FABRIC

1. Matching the wrong sides and selvage edges, fold the fabric in half lengthwise. Bringing the fold up to meet the selvages, fold it again so that you have 4 fabric layers. It's ok if the cut ends are not even, just make sure the folds lie flat and the bottom fold lines up with a horizontal line on the mat (**Fig. 12**).

Fig. 12

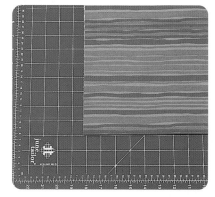

2. Place the right edge of your ruler just over the left end of the fabric, keeping the left edge of the ruler lined up with a vertical line on the mat (**Fig. 13**).

Fig. 13

3. Holding the rotary cutter at an angle, as shown in **Fig. 14**, place the side of the blade against the edge of the ruler. Make sure that none of your fingers are hanging over the side of the ruler where you will be cutting. Pressing down firmly, roll the cutter **away** from you along the edge of the ruler from the fold through the selvage.

Fig. 14

TIP

You might need to stop cutting about half way through a long cut and without moving the fabric or ruler, "walk" your hand up the ruler to keep the end of the ruler from slipping.

CUTTING A STRIP

1. Place the ruler over the cut edge of the fabric the measurement given in the project instructions. For example, if the instructions say cut a 3" strip, line up the 3" mark on the ruler with the cut edge of the fabric (**Fig. 15**)

Fig. 15

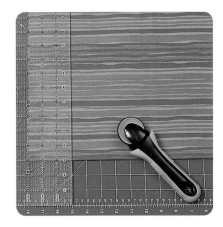

2. Make the cut as you did in Step 3 of **Squaring-Up The Fabric**, page 8. Repeat for each strip needed for your project.

TIP
After cutting several strips from a piece of fabric, you may need to re-square the edge as shown in **Figs. 13-14**.

CUTTING SQUARES OR RECTANGLES

1. To trim the selvages from your strips, unfold the strip so that you have two layers again. Referring to **Fig. 16**, place the folded strip on the mat with selvage ends to your right. Line up a horizontal mark on ruler with one long edge of the strip; make the cut. Turn the entire mat so that the cut end is to your left (**Fig. 17**).

Fig. 16

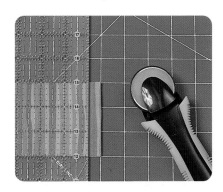

Fig. 17

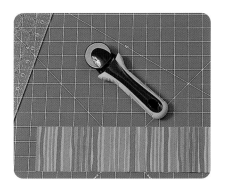

DID YOU KNOW?
The **dictionary defines** a quilt as a bed cover made of two layers of cloth filled with down, cotton, wool, etc. and stitched together in lines or patterns to keep the filling in place.

2. Place the ruler over the cut end of the fabric the measurement given in the project instructions. For example, if the instructions say cut a 3" x 3" square, line up the 3" vertical mark on the ruler with the cut edge of the fabric. Line up a horizontal mark on the ruler with one long edge of the strip (**Fig. 18**); make the cut. Repeat for the number of squares or rectangles needed.

Fig. 18

CUTTING BORDERS

Borders for large quilts are usually cut along the lengthwise grain of the fabric because it does not stretch as much as the crosswise grain.

1. Before cutting your borders, remove the selvages by placing the fabric on the mat with the selvages to your left and the squared-up end facing you. Place the ruler just over the left selvage and line up a horizontal mark on the mat with the squared-up end of the fabric (**Fig. 19**).

Fig. 19

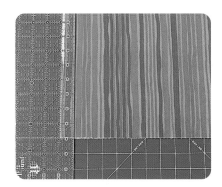

2. You may be cutting along a length of fabric that is longer than the mat so you may have to make the cuts in sections. Make the first cut the length of the mat and then move the next section of fabric to be cut onto the mat. Repeat until you have removed the selvages from the length of the fabric.

3. To cut the borders, place the ruler over the cut edge of the fabric the measurement given in the project instructions. For example, if the instructions say cut a 5" wide border, line up the 5" mark on the ruler with the cut edge of the fabric (**Fig. 20**). Make cuts as in Step 2, moving the next section of fabric onto mat as needed (**Fig. 21**).

Fig. 20

Fig. 21

PIECING

- When piecing, always stitch with an **exact** 1/4" seam allowance. The measurement from the needle to the outer edge of your presser foot should be 1/4".

- Presser feet that are exactly 1/4" wide are available for most sewing machines. If this is the case with your machine, your presser foot is your best guide.

- If your presser foot is not exactly 1/4" wide, measure 1/4" from the needle (a ruler or a piece of graph paper with a 1/4" grid makes a handy measuring tool) and mark the throat plate with a piece of masking tape (**Fig. 22**). You will use the tape as your seam guide.

Fig. 22

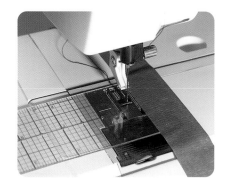

STITCHING

1. Set your sewing machine stitch length for approximately 11 stitches per inch. Place a new needle in your sewing machine.
2. Thread your machine and fill the bobbin. Practice stitching on scrap fabric until you are comfortable sewing straight, precise ¼" seams.
3. Place your first 2 pieces with right sides together and raw edges matching; pin the pieces together (**Fig. 23**).

Fig. 23

4. Hold the top and bobbin threads out of the way. Stopping to remove the pins just before they reach the sewing machine needle, sew the seam from edge to edge of your fabric (**Fig. 24**). It is not necessary to backstitch at the beginning or end of any seam that will be crossed by another seam.

Fig. 24

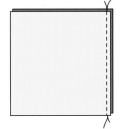

5. Guide (don't push) the fabric under the presser foot. Allow your machine to "feed" the fabric through.
6. Continue adding pieces, following your project instructions, until a unit, block, or row is completed.

SEWING ACROSS SEAM INTERSECTIONS

When joining units, sometimes you will need to sew across previously sewn seams.

1. Place the units right sides together and match the seams exactly, making sure the seam allowances are pressed in opposite directions (**Fig. 25**).

Fig. 25

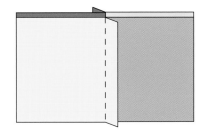

2. Place a pin on either side of the seam to hold the seam allowances in place.
3. Sew from edge to edge of the units. Open the pieces and make sure the seams meet exactly.

TRIMMING SEAM ALLOWANCES

When piecing, some seam allowances may extend beyond the edges of the sewn pieces. Trim away these "dog ears" that extend beyond the edges of the sewn pieces (**Fig. 26**).

Fig. 26

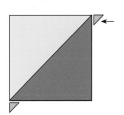

TIP
Sewing on the lines of a piece of graph paper, with no thread in your needle and bobbin, will help you to see if you are keeping your stitching lines straight.

11

PRESSING

- Use a steam iron set on "Cotton" for all pressing.
- Pressing is not the same as ironing because you do not slide the iron back and forth across the fabric. To press, lift the iron from one section to the next to keep from stretching the fabric.
- Pressing from the right side will help keep tucks from forming in the seam allowances.
- Seam allowances usually are pressed to one side toward the darker fabric.
- Always press as you go. When you sew a seam, press that seam.

QUILTING

Quilting holds the three layers (quilt top, batting, and backing) together. Because marking, preparing the backing, layering, and quilting are all a part of the quilting process, please read the entire **Quilting Section**, *pages 12-15, before beginning the quilting on your project.*

MARKING

- To have a guide line to follow for your quilting stitches, you can draw your quilting design on your Quilt Top with a fabric marking pencil.

- Strips of masking tape work well as a guide if you do not want to draw on your fabric; just stitch along the edge of the tape (**Fig. 27**).

Fig. 27

- Test your pencil on a scrap of fabric to make sure the marks can easily be washed out or brushed away.
- Refer to your project photo and quilting diagram for stitch placement. Using a ruler to help you draw straight lines, lightly draw the quilting lines on your Quilt Top.

BACKING

*For small quilts, cut your backing the size called for in the project instructions. For larger quilt tops (****Pinwheel Throw*** *and* ***Trip Around The World****) you will need to piece the backing by following Steps 1 – 4.*

1. Measure the length and width of your quilt top; add 4" to each measurement.

TIP
You can quilt your project as shown or draw a design of your own. When planning your quilting, keep in mind that straight lines are easier to quilt than curves.

TIP
When using an iron, remember to return the iron to an upright position and turn it off after you are finished pressing.

2. Cut 2 pieces of backing fabric the width of the fabric and slightly longer than the length measurement. Trim off the selvages.

3. Matching right sides, sew the long edges together, forming a tube (**Fig. 28**). Re-fold the tube so that the seams match; press along one fold (**Fig. 29**). Cut along pressed fold to form a single piece (**Fig. 30**).

Fig. 28

Fig. 29

Fig. 30

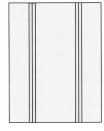

4. Trim the backing to the size called for in the project instructions and press the seam allowances open.

BATTING

Low-loft polyester batting is recommended for hand quilted projects. For a fluffier look and feel in tied quilts, you may want to use a medium-loft polyester batting. Polyester batting is easy to stitch through when hand quilting and will not shift and pull apart in tied quilts. Cut your batting the size called for in your project instructions.

LAYERING

1. Spread the backing, wrong side up, on a large table or on the floor. Use pieces of masking tape to hold the backing tight and smooth (**Fig. 31**).

Fig. 31

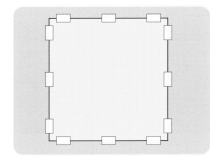

2. Place the batting on top of the backing and carefully smooth out all wrinkles.

3. Center the Quilt Top right side up on the batting and smooth out any wrinkles.

4. To pin-baste, start in the center of the quilt and work outward toward the edges using safety pins, placed about 4" apart, to pin the layers together (**Fig. 32**). Try not to place pins on top of any marked quilting lines. Remove the masking tape from the backing.

Fig. 32

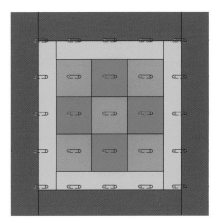

HAND QUILTING

You will be hand quilting using a ³/₈" long Running Stitch. The most important thing you will need to master when hand quilting is keeping your stitches straight and equal in length.

1. Always begin quilting in the center of the quilt and work toward the outside edges. If you are using a hoop, position your quilt with the quilt top facing you. Check the quilt top and backing to make sure they are smooth.

2. Thread a crewel needle with 2 strands of embroidery floss (cut about 20" long) in the color called for in your project instructions; knot 1 end.

TIP
You may find it easier to take 1 – 2 stitches at a time until you get used to rocking the needle to make the stitches or when quilting through a seam allowance.

3. Because you do not want knots to show on the top or bottom surface of your quilt, quilters use a technique called "popping" the knot. Insert the needle into the quilt top and batting (but not the backing) approximately ¹/₂" from where you wish to begin quilting. Bring the needle up through the quilt top at the point where you wish to begin quilting (**Fig. 33**); when knot catches on quilt top, give thread a quick, short pull to "pop" the knot through the quilt top and into the batting (**Fig. 34**).

Fig. 33

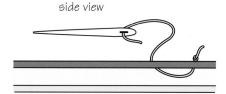

side view

Fig. 34

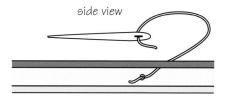

side view

4. Place your thimble on the middle finger of your sewing hand. Hold the needle in your sewing hand and place your other hand underneath the quilt where you will begin stitching. Let the hoop rest against your arm and in your lap. Use your thimble finger to push the needle down through all the layers.

5. When you feel the needle touch your underneath index finger, use that finger to push the tip of the needle back up through the layers.

6. Referring to **Fig. 35**, rock the needle up and down, taking 2 - 3 stitches before bringing the needle and floss completely through the layers. You can use the thumb of your sewing hand to push down the fabric in front of the needle as you stitch. Check the back of the quilt to make sure the stitches are going through all the layers.

Fig. 35

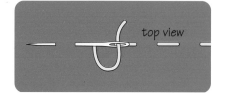

top view

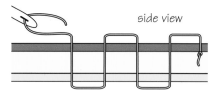

side view

7. When you reach the end of your thread, knot the thread close to the fabric and "pop" knot into the batting; clip the thread close to fabric and the end will sink between the layers.

8. Re-thread your needle and continue quilting, moving your hoop as needed, until you have finished quilting the project. Remove the basting pins.

FINISHING
MAKING A HANGING SLEEVE

Attaching a hanging sleeve to the back of your wall hanging or quilt before the binding is added allows you to display your completed project on a wall.

1. Measure the width across the top edge of your quilt and subtract 1". Cut a piece of fabric 7" wide by this measurement.

2. Press the short edges of the fabric piece $1/4$" to the wrong side; press the edges $1/4$" to the wrong side again and machine stitch in place.

3. Matching wrong sides, fold the piece in half lengthwise to form a tube.

4. Follow your project instructions and **Binding** to sew the binding to the top and bottom edges of your quilt and to trim the backing and batting. **Before** blind stitching the binding to backing, match the raw edges, center and sew the hanging sleeve to the top edge on back of your quilt.

5. Finish binding your quilt, treating the hanging sleeve as part of the backing.

6. Blindstitch (**Fig. 38**, page 16) the bottom of the hanging sleeve to the backing, taking care not to stitch through to the front of your quilt.

BINDING

1. Cut crosswise strips of binding fabric the width called for in your project instructions. With right sides together, sew the short ends of the strips together to make one long length of binding.

2. Press the seam allowances open. Matching wrong sides and raw edges, press the binding in half lengthwise.

3. Measure the width of your *quilt top* (not including the batting or backing); add 1". Cut 2 lengths of binding this measurement.

ADDING A LABEL
Your quilt is a work of art and you can sign and date it, just like an artist would a painting, by making a label to sew onto the backing.

- Cut a square, about 6" x 6", from muslin or a light colored scrap of fabric from your quilt top.

- Use a fine-point permanent fabric marker to write your name, the date you made the quilt, and any special reasons you made it (for example, it was made to be a gift).

- You could decorate the label with colored fabric markers or some embroidery stitches.

- Press under each raw edge $1/4$" to the wrong side; pin and then blindstitch (**Fig. 38**, page 16) the label to the back of your quilt.

4. Matching right sides and raw edges of the quilt top and binding, center and then pin binding to the top and bottom edges of the quilt. The binding will extend ½" past the corners of the quilt top. Sew the binding to the quilt (**Fig. 36**).

Fig. 36

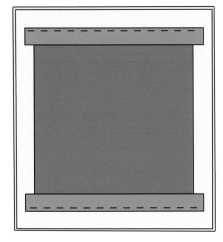

5. Trim the top and bottom edges of the backing and batting ¼" larger than the quilt top.

6. Trim the ends of the binding even with the edges of the quilt top. Fold the binding over to the quilt backing and pin the pressed edges in place, covering your stitching line (**Fig. 37**).

Fig. 37

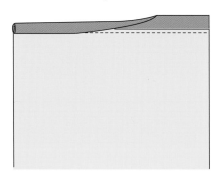

7. Blindstitch the binding to the backing, taking care not to stitch through to front of quilt. To blindstitch, come up at 1, go down at 2, and come up at 3 (**Fig. 38**).

Fig. 38

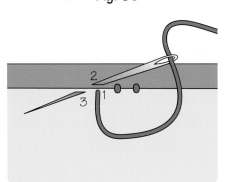

8. Measure the length of your *quilt top* (including the top and bottom binding); add 3". Cut 2 lengths of binding this measurement.

9. Matching right sides and raw edges of the quilt top and binding, center and then pin binding to the side edges of the quilt (**Fig. 39**). The binding will extend 1½" past the corners of the quilt. Sew the binding to the quilt. Trim the backing and batting as you did in **Step 5**.

Fig. 39

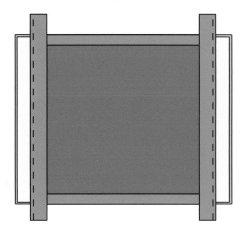

10. Trim each binding end so that it extends ½" past the corners of the quilt. Fold each binding end over to the quilt backing (**Fig. 40**); pin in place. Fold binding over to the quilt backing and blindstitch the binding in place, taking care not to stitch through to the front of the quilt.

Fig. 40

Now you are ready to start on your project! Your project instructions may refer you back to sections of the General Instructions for specific steps.

SEWING CADDY

Make this handy sewing caddy for storing your supplies while learning how to make and use templates, layer a quilt "sandwich", and appliqué using an overcast stitch.

Finished Size Folded:
9" x 5½" (23 cm x 14 cm)
Finished Size Open:
9" x 14" (23 cm x 36 cm)

MATERIALS

Refer to **What You Need**, page 4, and **Fabrics**, page 5, to help you select your supplies and prepare your fabrics. Yardage amounts are based on using 43/44" (109/112 cm) wide fabric.

> ½ yd (46 cm) of hot pink and white stripe
> ⅜ yd (57 cm) of multi-colored stripe

You will also need:
> Light pink embroidery floss
> ½ yd (46 cm) of ⅜" (9.5 mm) wide hot pink grosgrain ribbon
> Scrap of hot pink felt
> 1½" (38mm) long safety pins
> 9" x 14" (23 cm x 36 cm) rectangle of low-loft batting

CUTTING OUT THE PIECES

Depending on your chosen cutting method, follow either **Scissor Cutting**, page 6, or **Rotary Cutting**, page 8, to cut pieces A & B. Refer to **Making and Using Templates**, page 6, to use appliqué patterns C & D, page 21.

From hot pink and white stripe:
- If **scissor cutting**, cut 2 rectangles 9" x 14" (**A**).
  If **rotary cutting**, cut 1 strip 14" wide. From this strip, cut 2 rectangles 9" x 14" (**A**).

From multi-colored stripe:
- If **scissor cutting**, cut 1 rectangle 9" x 17" (**B**).
  If **rotary cutting**, cut 1 strip 9" wide. From this strip, cut 1 rectangle 9" x 17" (**B**).

From hot pink felt:
- Cut 1 needle holder (**C**).
- Cut 1 heart (**D**).

MAKING THE SEWING CADDY

Follow **Piecing**, page 10, and **Pressing**, page 12, to make the Sewing Caddy.

MAKING THE INNER PANEL

1. Matching short ends and wrong sides, fold **B** in half to find the center of the rectangle. Mark the center by placing a straight pin at the fold line on each edge; unfold (**Fig. 1**). With the wrong side facing up, fold each short end to meet at the pins (**Fig. 2**). Press the folds.

Fig. 1

Fig. 2

2. Turn **B** over, center and pin the needle holder ¹/₂" from the top edge (**Fig. 3**). Use 6 strands of floss and refer to the **Overcast Diagram** to appliqué the needle holder by making evenly spaced diagonal stitches over the edges of the needle holder.

Fig. 3

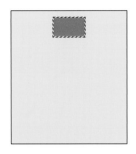

Overcast Diagram

3. Layer one **A**, right side up, and **B**, appliquéd side up, as shown in **Fig. 4**. The bottom fold of **B** should be ¹/₂" from the bottom edge of **A** and the side edges should be even. Pin layers together.

Fig. 4

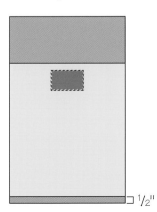
¹/₂"

4. To make the large pocket, machine stitch 4¹/₂" from the bottom fold, across the width of **B**. To make the two small pockets, stitch down the center of **B** from the seam to the bottom edge to complete the Inner Panel (**Fig. 5**).

Fig. 5

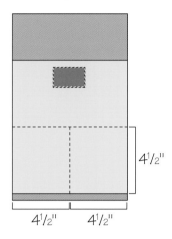
4¹/₂"
4¹/₂" 4¹/₂"

5. Cut the ribbon into two 9" long pieces. Overlapping the edge by ¹/₂", center one end of a ribbon piece on the wrong side of the Inner Panel along the top edge. Pin the ribbon in place. Sew the ribbon to the Inner Panel using a machine straight stitch (**Fig. 6**). Set inner panel aside.

Fig. 6

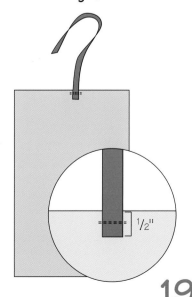
¹/₂"

19

MAKING THE OUTER PANEL

1. To appliqué the heart, refer to **Fig. 7** for placement and pin the heart to the right side of the remaining rectangle **A**. Using 6 strands of floss, Overcast around the edges of the heart.

Fig. 7

2. Center the remaining ribbon piece 3" from the edge on the right side of **A** with raw edge of ribbon facing bottom edge of **A**. Pin the ribbon in place. Using a machine straight stitch, sew the ribbon to **A** to complete the Outer Panel (**Fig. 8**).

Fig. 8

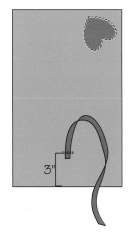

LAYERING AND FINISHING

1. To layer the sewing caddy, place Outer Panel, right side down, the batting, and then the Inner Panel, right side up. Use safety pins, placed about 3"-4" apart, to pin the layers together. Using 4 strands of floss, overcast around the outer edges, through all the layers (**Fig. 9**).

Fig. 9

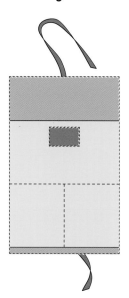

2. Refer to **Sewing Caddy Diagram** to fold the bottom edge of the caddy along the horizontal stitching line. Fold top edge of caddy over 3¼" and tie the ribbons into a bow.

Sewing Caddy Diagram

Fill your Sewing Caddy with embroidery scissors, a thimble, thread, and a package of needles and you will be ready to start on your next project!

Needle Holder
C

Heart
D

21

LESSON 2

FLOOR PILLOW COVER

A large purchased pillow takes on a jazzy new look when you tie on a quilted cover. Learn how to piece, layer a quilt "sandwich", use buttons to "quilt" the layers, and stitch a mock-binding while making this fast and easy project.

Finished Floor Pillow Cover Size:
22" x 22" (61 cm x 61 cm)

MATERIALS

Refer to **What You Need**, page 4, and **Fabrics**, page 5, to help you select your supplies and prepare your fabrics. Yardage amounts are based on using 43/44" (109/112 cm) wide fabric.

> 1/4 yd (23 cm) of pink floral
> 1/8 yd (11 cm) of purple polka dot
> 1/4 yd (23 cm) of green print
> 2 1/2 yds (2.3 m) of pink polka dot

You will also need:

> Small sticky-notes
> Pink embroidery floss
> 4 pink 7/8" (22 mm) diameter 2-hole buttons
> 4 orange 3/8" (10 mm) diameter 2-hole buttons
> 8 yds (7.3 m) of 5/8" (16 mm) wide fuchsia grosgrain ribbon
> 1 1/2" (38 mm) long safety pins
> 22" x 22" (56 cm x 56 cm) square of low-loft batting
> 24" x 24" (61 cm x 61 cm) purchased pillow

CUTTING OUT THE PIECES

Using a sticky-note for each letter, write the letters A-I on the notes. As you cut, keep the fabric pieces organized by labeling pieces with their matching letter. Depending on your chosen cutting method, follow either **Scissor Cutting**, page 6, or **Rotary Cutting**, page 8, to cut pieces A-I.

From pink floral:

- If **scissor cutting**, cut 1 square 6 1/2" x 6 1/2" (**A**). If **rotary cutting**, cut 1 strip 6 1/2" wide. From this strip, cut 1 square 6 1/2" x 6 1/2" (**A**).

From purple polka dot:

- If **scissor cutting**, cut 2 rectangles 2 1/2" x 6 1/2" (**B**) and 2 rectangles 2 1/2" x 10 1/2" (**C**). If **rotary cutting**, cut 1 strip 2 1/2" wide. From this strip, cut 2 rectangles 2 1/2" x 6 1/2" (**B**) and 2 rectangles 2 1/2" x 10 1/2" (**C**).

From green print:

- If **scissor cutting**, cut 2 rectangles 3 1/2" x 10 1/2" (**D**) and 2 rectangles 3 1/2" x 16 1/2" (**E**). If **rotary cutting**, cut 2 strips 3 1/2" wide. From these strips, cut 2 rectangles 3 1/2" x 10 1/2" (**D**) and 2 rectangles 3 1/2" x 16 1/2". (**E**).

From pink polka dot:

- If **scissor cutting**, cut 2 rectangles 3 1/2" x 16 1/2" (**F**) and 2 rectangles 3 1/2" x 22 1/2" (**G**). If **rotary cutting**, cut 3 strips 3 1/2" wide. From these strips, cut 2 rectangles 3 1/2" x 16 1/2" (**F**) and 2 rectangles 3 1/2" x 22 1/2" (**G**).

- Cut 1 backing square 24" x 24" (**H**).

- Cut 2 squares 22 1/2" x 22 1/2" (**I**).

MAKING THE FLOOR PILLOW COVER FRONT

*Follow **Piecing**, page 10, and **Pressing**, page 12, to make the Floor Pillow Cover. Use a 1/4" seam allowance for all sewing.*

1. Matching right sides and raw edges, sew 1 **B** rectangle to 1 **A** square as shown in **Fig. 1**. Press the seam allowances toward **B**. Sew the remaining **B** rectangle to the opposite side of the **A** square to make **Unit 1**.

Fig. 1

Unit 1

2. Sew a **C** rectangle to the top and bottom of Unit 1 to make **Unit 2**.

Unit 2

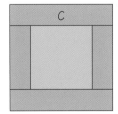

3. Sew a **D** rectangle to the left side and right sides of Unit 2 to make **Unit 3**.

Unit 3

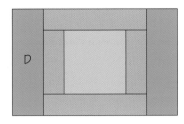

4. Sew an **E** rectangle to the top and bottom of Unit 3 to make **Unit 4**.

Unit 4

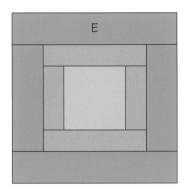

5. Sew an **F** rectangle to the left and right sides of Unit 4 to make **Unit 5**.

Unit 5

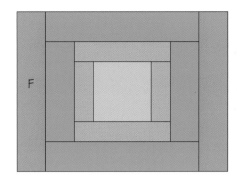

6. Sew a **G** rectangle to the top and bottom edges of Unit 5 to make **Floor Pillow Cover Front**.

Floor Pillow Cover Front

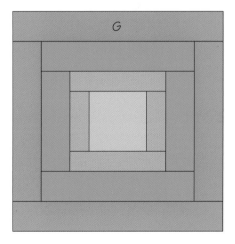

DID YOU KNOW?
Crusaders brought the art of quilting to Europe from the Middle East in the late 11th century. Knights wore quilted garments under their armor for padding.

LAYERING AND QUILTING

*Refer to photo and **Pillow Cover Finishing Diagram**, while making the Pillow Cover.*

1. Layer the backing square **H**, right side down, batting, and the Floor Pillow Cover Front, right side up. Backing will be 1" larger than Pillow Cover Front on all sides (**Fig. 2**).

Fig. 2

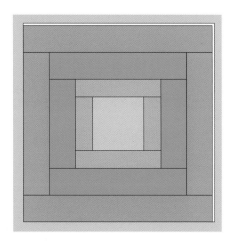

2. Placing safety pins about 4 inches apart, pin the 3 layers together.
3. To make the mock-binding, fold and press each raw edge of the backing ½" to the wrong side of the fabric.
4. Covering the raw edges of the pillow cover front, make a second ½" fold; pin the folded edges in place.

5. Use 3 strands of pink floss to make a Running Stitch (**Fig. 35**, page 14) through all the layers, about ⅛" from the inner folded edges.
6. Place an orange button on top of a pink button. Sew through the holes in both buttons to attach them to the Pillow Cover Front.

MAKING THE FLOOR PILLOW COVER BACK

1. Leaving a 5" opening for turning along one edge, match the right sides and raw edges to sew the two **I** squares together (**Fig. 3**).

Fig. 3

5"

2. Being careful not to cut the stitching, clip the corners as shown in **Fig. 4**. Turn squares right side out and press. Stitch the opening closed by hand to make the **Pillow Cover Back**.

Fig. 4

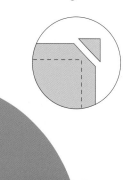

FINISHING

1. Cut the ribbon into 16 pieces, each 18" long.
2. Refer to **Fig. 5** for ribbon placement. Fold and press under one raw end of each ribbon piece ½". Overlapping the edges by ½", pin pressed end of each ribbon piece to the wrong side of the Pillow Cover Front and Pillow Cover Back.

Fig. 5

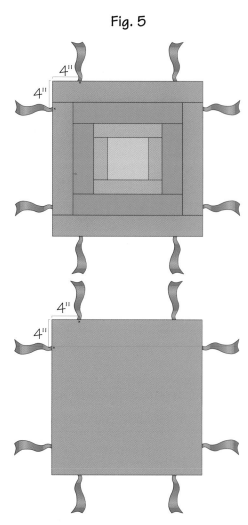

4"

4"

4"

4"

3. Sew the ribbons to the Pillow Cover Front and Pillow Cover Back using a small hand stitch (**Fig. 6**).

Fig. 6

4. Place your pillow between the Pillow Cover Front and Back. Tie each pair of ribbons into a bow at the sides of the pillow.

Pillow Cover Finishing Diagram

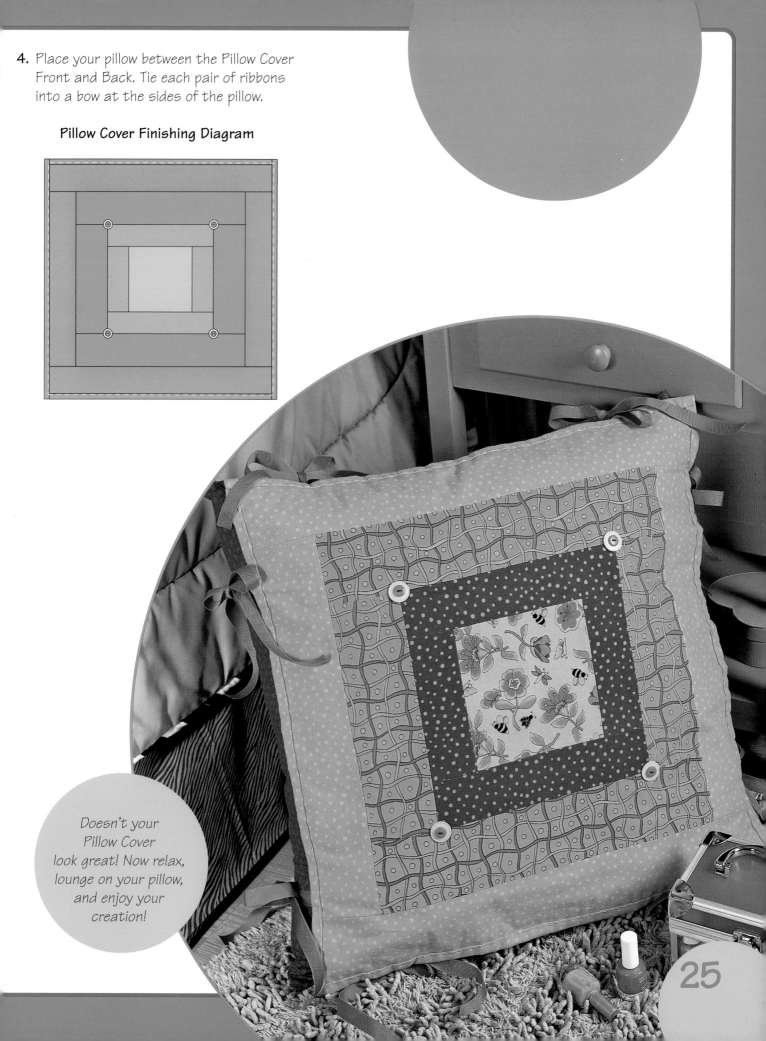

Doesn't your Pillow Cover look great! Now relax, lounge on your pillow, and enjoy your creation!

PILLOW WITH PHOTO TRANSERS

Gather some awesome fabrics, a handful of cute buttons, and a couple of your favorite photos to make this totally cool pillow. You will learn how to piece a block, add sashings and borders, layer a quilt "sandwich", and hand quilt.

Finished Pillow Size:
18" x 18" (46 cm x 46 cm)
Finished Block Size:
6" x 6" (15 cm x 15 cm)

MATERIALS

Refer to **What You Need**, page 4, and **Fabrics**, page 5, to help you select your supplies and prepare your fabrics. Yardage amounts are based on using 43/44" (109/112 cm) wide fabric.

$^3/_4$ yd (69 cm) of white solid
$^1/_8$ yd (11 cm) of orange print
$^1/_8$ yd (11 cm) of yellow solid
$^7/_8$ yd (80 cm) of multi-colored stripe

You will also need:
Small sticky-notes
Assorted buttons
Yellow and pink embroidery
 floss
Photo transfer paper
Black fine-point permanent
 fabric marker
$1^1/_2$" (38mm) long safety pins
18" x 18" (46 cm x 46 cm)
 pillow form
$22^1/_2$" x $22^1/_2$" (57 cm x 57 cm)
 square of low-loft batting

CUTTING OUT THE PIECES

Using a sticky-note for each letter, write the letters A-G on the notes. As you cut, keep the fabric pieces organized by labeling pieces with their matching letter. If using scissors to cut fabric, follow **Scissor Cutting**, page 6, to cut large shapes A, F, & G and to use patterns B-F, pages 30-31. If using a rotary cutter to cut fabric, follow **Rotary Cutting**, page 8, to cut pieces A-G.

From white solid:
- If **scissor cutting**, cut 1 pillow top backing $22^1/_2$" x $22^1/_2$" (**A**) and 2 squares (**B**).
  If **rotary cutting**, cut 1 strip $22^1/_2$" wide. From this strip, cut 1 pillow top backing $22^1/_2$" x $22^1/_2$" (**A**) and 2 squares $7^1/_2$" x $7^1/_2$" (**B**).

From orange print:
- If **scissor cutting**, cut 4 rectangles (**C**).
  If **rotary cutting**, cut 1 strip $2^1/_2$" wide. From this strip, cut 4 rectangles $2^1/_2$" x $6^1/_2$" (**C**).

From yellow solid:
- If **scissor cutting**, cut 4 border squares (**D**) and 2 rectangles (**E**).
  If **rotary cutting**, cut 1 strip $2^3/_4$" wide. From this strip, cut 4 border squares $2^3/_4$" x $2^3/_4$" (**D**) and 2 rectangles $2^1/_2$" x $6^1/_2$" (**E**).

From multi-colored stripe:
- If **scissor cutting**, cut 2 vertical sashings (**F**) and 1 horizontal sashing 2" x 14" (**G**).
  If **rotary cutting**, cut 1 strip 2" wide. From this strip, cut 2 vertical sashings 2" x $6^1/_2$" (**F**) and 1 horizontal sashing 2" x 14" (**G**).
- If **scissor cutting**, cut 4 borders $2^3/_4$" x 17" (**H**).
  If **rotary cutting**, cut 2 strips $2^3/_4$" wide. From these strips, cut 4 borders $2^3/_4$" x 17" (**H**).
- Cut 1 pillow back $18^1/_2$" x $18^1/_2$" (**I**).

MAKING THE PHOTO BLOCKS

Manufacturer's instructions for using photo transfer paper will be different depending on the brand of paper you use. Be sure to carefully read and follow their instructions.

1. Print or copy your photos onto the photo transfer paper.
2. Cut out the images and transfer one image to the center of each **B** square.
3. Centering the images, trim the squares to $6^1/_2$" x $6^1/_2$" to make 2 **photo blocks**.

MAKING THE PILLOW TOP

Follow **Piecing**, page 10, and **Pressing**, page 12, to make the Pillow Top. Use a 1/4" seam allowance for all sewing.

1. Matching right sides and raw edges, sew one **C** rectangle to one **E** rectangle as shown in **Fig. 1**. Press the seam allowances toward the darker fabric. Sew a second **C** rectangle to the opposite side of the **E** rectangle and press to make **Unit 1**. Make 2 Unit 1's.

Fig. 1

Unit 1 (make 2)

2. Sew 1 **photo block**, 1 **F** sashing, and 1 **Unit 1** together to make **Row A**.

Row A

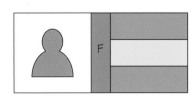

3. Sew **1 Unit 1**, 1 **F** sashing, and 1 **photo block** together to make **Row B**.

Row B

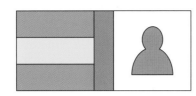

4. Sew Rows A and B and the **G** sashing together to make the **Pillow Top Center**.

Pillow Top Center

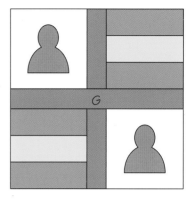

27

ADDING THE BORDERS

The borders are cut longer than needed to allow for differences in sewing. Following the steps below, measure and trim the borders to the correct length.

1. Measure the length through the middle of the Pillow Top Center. Trim 2 of the **H** borders to this measurement. Sew 1 **H** border to each side of the Pillow Top Center (**Fig. 2**).

Fig. 2

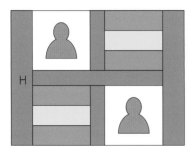

2. Measure the width through the middle of the Pillow Top center, excluding the side borders; add ¹/₂" for seam allowances. Trim the 2 remaining **H** borders to this measurement. Sew a **D** square to each end of an **H** border to make the **top border** (**Fig. 3**).

Fig. 3

3. Repeat Step 2 using the second **H** border to make the **bottom border**. Referring to the **Pillow Top Diagram**, sew the top and bottom borders to the Pillow Top Center to finish piecing the **Pillow Top**.

QUILTING AND EMBELLISHING

*Refer to the photo and the **Pillow Top Diagram**, page 29, for placement of the quilting.*

1. Follow **Quilting**, page 12, to mark, layer, pin-baste, and quilt your Pillow Top, using pillow top backing **A**. We used 3 strands of pink embroidery floss for all quilting. Our pillow top has a straight line of quilting through the center of each sashing. There is outline quilting in the borders, ¹/₄" away from the inner seams.

2. Arrange your buttons on your photo blocks until you are pleased with the placement. Sew the buttons to the Pillow Top. Add Cross Stitches (**Fig. 4**) where you desire using 3 strands of yellow embroidery floss.

Fig. 4

3. Using the black fabric marker, you can write a name or tell something about each photo in the yellow rectangle beside it.

FINISHING

1. Matching right sides and raw edges, pin the Pillow Top and pillow back **I** together.

2. Leaving a 14" opening across the bottom edge for turning, sew pieces together (**Fig. 5**).

Fig. 5

14"

3. Being careful not to cut the stitching, clip corners as shown in **Fig. 6**. Turn the Pillow Cover to the right side and press.

Fig. 6

4. Insert the pillow form into the Pillow Cover and hand stitch the opening closed.

Pillow Top Diagram

Wow! That was so easy and fun to make. Your pillow will look really cool in your room displayed on the bed or in a chair.

B

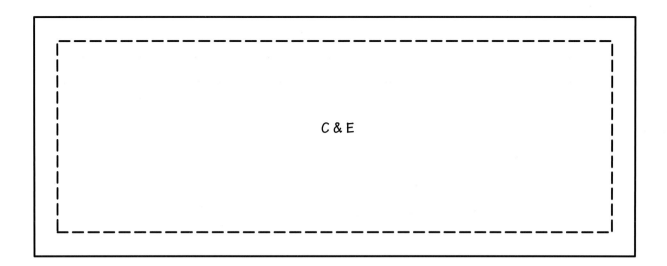

C & E

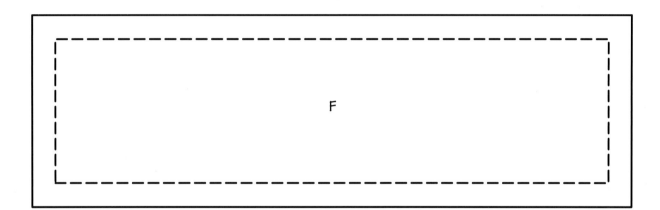

F

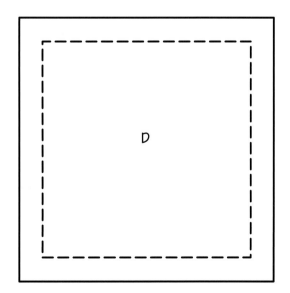

D

LESSON 4

QUILT AS YOU GO TOTE BAG

They're everywhere — tote bags and purses are all the rage! Roomy enough to carry all your gear, this really cool looking tote is also a lot of fun to make. Learn how to use fusible batting, the "stitch and flip" sewing method, and how to bind.

Finished Tote Bag Size:
12" x 14" (30 cm x 36 cm)

MATERIALS

Refer to **What You Need**, page 4, and **Fabrics**, page 5, to help you select your supplies and prepare your fabrics. Yardage amounts are based on using 43/44" (109/112 cm) wide fabric.

$1/8$ yd (11 cm) **each** of 8 assorted bright prints
$5/8$ yd (57 cm) of black and white check

You will also need:
$1\frac{1}{2}$ yds (1.4 m) of 1" (25 mm) wide black web belting for handles
4 assorted bright-colored buttons $3/4$" (19 mm) diameter
4 assorted bright-colored buttons 1" (25 mm) diameter
$14\frac{1}{2}$" x $24\frac{1}{2}$" (37 cm x 62 cm) rectangle of low-loft fusible fleece

CUTTING OUT THE PIECES

Depending on your chosen cutting method, follow either **Scissor Cutting**, page 6, or **Rotary Cutting**, page 8, to cut pieces A-C.

From each of the 8 assorted bright prints:
- If **scissor cutting**, cut 1 rectangle $3\frac{1}{2}$" x $14\frac{1}{2}$" (**A**). If **rotary cutting**, cut 1 strip $3\frac{1}{2}$" wide. From this strip, cut 1 rectangle $3\frac{1}{2}$" x $14\frac{1}{2}$" (**A**).

From black and white check:
- If **scissor cutting**, cut 1 lining rectangle $14\frac{1}{2}$" x $24\frac{1}{2}$" (**B**). If **rotary cutting**, cut 1 strip $14\frac{1}{2}$" wide. From this strip, cut 1 lining rectangle $14\frac{1}{2}$" x $24\frac{1}{2}$" (**B**).
- Cut 1 binding strip $2\frac{1}{2}$" x $24\frac{1}{2}$" (**C**).

MAKING THE TOTE BAG

Follow **Piecing**, page 10, and **Pressing**, page 12, to make the Tote Bag. Use a ¼" seam allowance for all sewing.

FUSING THE FLEECE AND LINING

Instructions for using fusible fleece may vary depending on the brand of fleece you use. Be sure to carefully read and follow your manufacturer's instructions.

1. With right (fusible) side facing up, place fleece on your ironing board. Gently smooth out any wrinkles, being careful not to tear or distort the shape of the fleece.
2. With right side facing up and matching raw edges, place lining rectangle **B** on top of fleece. Follow manufacturer's instructions to fuse lining and fleece.

STITCH AND FLIP

1. Matching top, bottom, and left edges, place an **A** rectangle (right side up) and a second **A** rectangle (right side down) on fleece. Sew through all the layers, ¼" from the right edge of rectangles (**Fig. 1**).

Fig. 1

2. "Flip" open the second **A** rectangle and press along the seam (**Fig. 2**).

Fig. 2

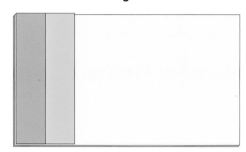

3. Refer to **Fig. 3** to position the third **A** rectangle; sew, flip, and press.

Fig. 3

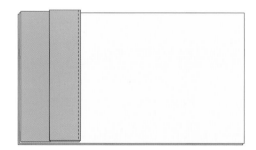

4. Continue adding **A** rectangles until you have sewn all 8 **A** rectangles to the lining and fleece. Using a long machine stitch, baste through all layers close to the raw edges on both short ends (**Fig. 4**).

Fig. 4

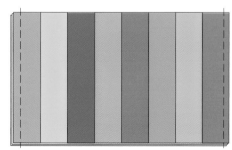

5. Matching right sides and short ends, fold the pieced panel in half. Sew side and bottom edges. Do not sew across top edge (**Fig. 5**).

Fig. 5

6. Being careful not to cut the stitching, clip corners as shown in **Fig. 6**. Turn the **tote bag** to the right side and press.

Fig. 6

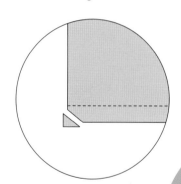

BINDING THE TOP EDGE

1. Matching right sides sew the short ends of binding strip **C** together to make a binding loop. Press the seam allowance open. Matching wrong sides and raw edges, fold the binding loop in half lengthwise and press (**Fig. 7**).

Fig. 7

2. Place the binding loop around the outside of the tote and match the raw edges of the binding loop with the raw edges of the tote bag. Using a $1/2$" seam allowance, stitch binding loop to tote bag (**Fig. 8**).

Fig. 8

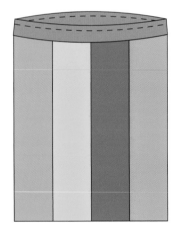

3. Fold the binding over the top edge of the tote bag, covering the stitching line and pin in place. Blindstitch(**Fig. 38**, page 16) the folded edge to the inside of the tote bag.

FINISHING

1. Cut two 26" long pieces of web belting.
2. Fold under each end of one handle 2" and pin. Center the folded handle ends over the seams on one side of the tote bag as shown in **Tote Bag Diagram** and pin in place.
3. Sewing through both thicknesses of the handle and through all the layers of the tote, sew 2 buttons to each handle end.
4. Repeat Steps 2 and 3 to sew the second handle to the opposite side of the tote bag.

Tote Bag Diagram

Your Tote Bag is finished! Fill it with your gear to be ready for school, a sleepover, or a day of fun!

LESSON 5

PILLOW TOPPER

Using really cool fabrics to match your bedspread, make a Pillow Topper to lay over the pillows on your bed. You will learn how to piece a traditional 9-patch block, add sashings and borders, layer a quilt "sandwich", and hand quilt.

Finished Topper Size:
55" x 27" (140 cm x 69 cm)

Finished Block Size:
12" x 12" (30 cm x 30 cm)

MATERIALS

Refer to **What You Need**, page 4, and **Fabrics**, page 5, to help you select your supplies and prepare your fabrics. Yardage amounts are based on using 43/44" (109/112 cm) wide fabric.

$^3/_8$ yd (34 cm) of pink polka dot
$^3/_8$ yd (34 cm) of green polka dot
$1^1/_4$ yds (1.1 m) of orange polka dot
$1^3/_4$ yds (1.6 m) of purple polka dot
$1^3/_4$ yds (1.6 m) of backing fabric

You will also need:
Green, orange, and purple embroidery floss
$1^1/_2$" (38 mm) long safety pins
62" x 34" (157 cm x 86 cm) rectangle of low-loft batting

CUTTING OUT THE PIECES

If using scissors to cut fabrics, follow **Scissor Cutting**, page 6, to use patterns A & B, page 39, and to cut large pieces C-H. If using a rotary cutter to cut fabrics, follow **Rotary Cutting**, page 8, to cut pieces A-H.

From pink polka dot:
- If **scissor cutting**, cut 15 squares (**A**).
  If **rotary cutting**, cut 2 strips $4^1/_2$" wide. From these strips, cut 15 squares $4^1/_2$" x $4^1/_2$" (**A**).

From green polka dot:
- If **scissor cutting**, cut 12 squares (**B**).
  If **rotary cutting**, cut 2 strips $4^1/_2$" wide. From these strips, cut 12 squares $4^1/_2$" x $4^1/_2$" (**B**).

From orange polka dot:
- Cut 2 *lengthwise* top and bottom inner borders $2^1/_2$" x $42^1/_2$" (**C**).
- Cut 2 *lengthwise* side inner borders $2^1/_2$" x $18^1/_2$" (**D**).
- Cut 2 sashing strips $2^1/_2$" x $12^1/_2$" (**E**).

From purple polka dot:
- Cut 5 binding strips $2^1/_2$" x 40" (**H**).
- Cut 2 *lengthwise* top and bottom outer borders $5^1/_2$" x $46^1/_2$" (**F**).
- Cut 2 *lengthwise* side outer borders $5^1/_2$" x $28^1/_2$" (**G**).

MAKING THE NINE-PATCH BLOCKS

Follow **Piecing**, page 10, and **Pressing**, page 12, to make the Pillow Topper. Use a $^1/_4$" seam allowance for all sewing.

1. Matching right sides and raw edges, sew an **A** square to a **B** square as shown in **Fig. 1**. Press seam allowances toward the **B** square. Sew another **A** square to the opposite side of the **B** square to make **Unit 1**. Make 6 Unit 1's.

Fig. 1

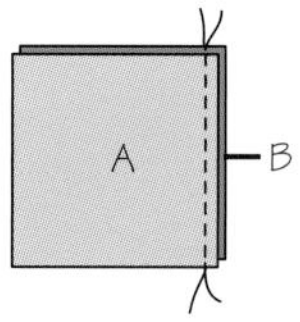

Unit 1 (make 6)

2. Repeat Step 1 to sew a **B** square to each side of an **A** square to make **Unit 2**. Make 3 Unit 2's.

Unit 2 (make 3)

3. Sew a Unit 1, a Unit 2, and another Unit 1 together to make a **Nine-Patch Block**. Make 3 Nine-Patch Blocks.

Nine-Patch Block (make 3)

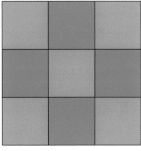

MAKING THE TOPPER CENTER

*Refer to the **Pillow Topper Diagram**, page 39, to assemble the Topper Center.*

1. Matching right sides and raw edges, sew a sashing strip **E** to the right side of a Nine-Patch Block to make **Unit 3**. Repeat to make another Unit 3.

Unit 3 (make 2)

2. Sew the 2 Unit 3's and the remaining Nine-Patch Block together to complete the **Topper Center**.

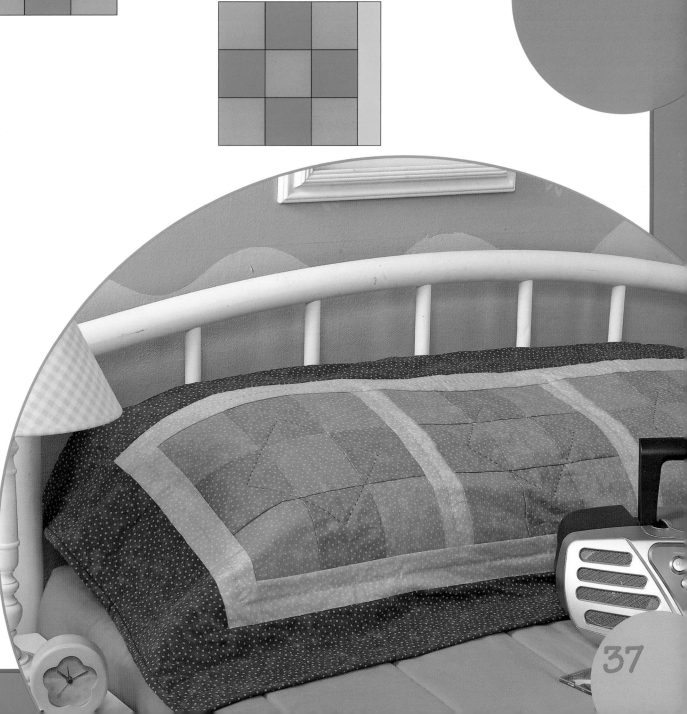

ADDING THE BORDERS

The borders are cut longer than needed to allow for differences in sewing. Following the steps below, measure and trim the borders to the correct length before sewing them to your Topper Center.

1. Measure the **width** through the middle of the Topper Center and trim the top and bottom inner borders C to this measurement (**Fig. 2**).

Fig. 2

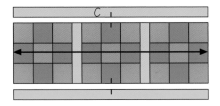

2. Mark the center of each edge of the Topper Center. Mark the center of each top and bottom inner border.

3. With right sides together, match and pin the top and bottom inner borders to the Topper Center at the center marks and corners, easing in any extra length. Sew the top and bottom inner borders to the Topper Center.

4. Measure the **length** through the middle of the Topper Center, including the top and bottom inner borders and trim the side inner borders D to this measurement. Mark the center of each side inner border (**Fig. 3**).

Fig. 3

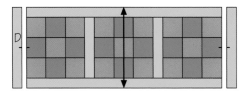

5. With right sides together, match and pin the side inner borders to the Topper Center at the center marks and corners, easing in any extra length (**Fig. 4**). Sew the side inner borders to the Topper Center.

Fig. 4

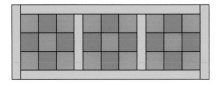

6. Repeat Steps 2 and 3 to measure, trim and sew the outer borders (**F** & **G**) to the Topper Center to complete your **Quilt Top**.

QUILTING AND FINISHING

1. Follow **Quilting**, page 12, to mark, layer, and quilt the Quilt Top. Refer to the **Quilting Diagram** to quilt a diamond in each Nine-Patch Block using 2 strands of green embroidery floss. Quilt a straight line through the center of the inner borders and sashings using 2 strands of orange embroidery floss. Quilt 2 straight, parallel lines in the outer borders using 2 strands of purple floss.

2. Follow **Finishing**, page 15, to bind, using binding strips **H**, and label your Pillow Topper.

That was so quick and easy, why not make a matching one to use as a table runner on a dresser or chest of drawers!

Pillow Topper Diagram

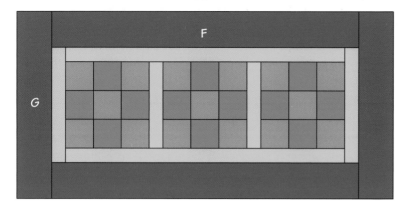

Quilting Diagram

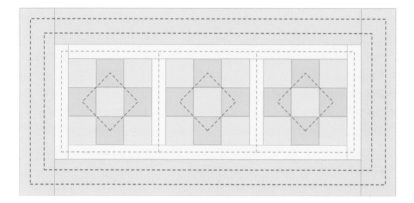

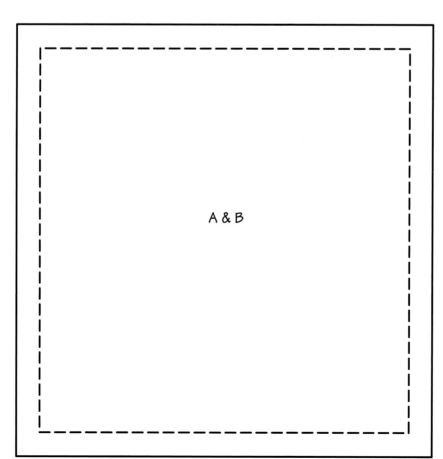

A & B

LESSON 6

TRIP AROUND THE WORLD THROW

Pick really cool fabrics in your favorite colors and use your creative talents to design your own quilt top while making this colorful throw. Learn how to plan and follow a quilt layout, layer a quilt "sandwich", pin baste, and tie a quilt.

Finished Quilt Size:
55" x 55" (140 cm x 140 cm)

Finished Block Size:
6" x 6" (15 cm x 15 cm)

MATERIALS

Refer to **What You Need**, page 4, and **Fabrics**, page 5, to help you select your supplies and prepare your fabrics. Yardage amounts are based on using 43/44" (109/112 cm) wide fabric.

$^7/_8$ yd (80 cm) **each** of 4 different print fabrics
$^1/_2$ yd (46 cm) of binding fabric
$3^1/_2$ yds (3.2 m) of backing fabric

You will also need:
Graph paper (optional)
Approximately 16 yds of sport-weight yarn
$1^1/_2$" (38 mm) long safety pins
62" x 62" (157 cm x 157 cm) square of batting

PLANNING YOUR QUILT

By working on paper before cutting your fabrics, you can arrange and re-arrange colors until you find just the right look! To make the Trip Around the World design, use like fabric for each letter on your Quilt Top Layout.

1. Photocopy the **Quilt Top Layout**, page 44, or draw the layout on graph paper. You will need 2 or 3 copies.
2. Our quilt uses 4 different fabrics. You can buy your fabrics and then design your quilt, or you can choose your favorite colors, decide on color placement, and then find fabrics to match.
3. Trying different color arrangements until you are happy with your plan, use colored pencils to color the squares on your layout.
4. Assign each fabric a letter **A-D** to match its placement on your layout.

CUTTING OUT THE PIECES

Depending on your chosen cutting method, follow either **Scissor Cutting**, page 6, to use patterns A-D, page 45, and to cut large piece E, or **Rotary Cutting**, page 8, to cut pieces A-E.

From each print fabric:
- If **scissor cutting**, cut 21 A squares. Repeat to cut 20 **B**, 20 **C**, and 20 **D** squares. If **rotary cutting**, cut 4 strips $6^1/_2$"wide. From these strips, cut 21 squares **A** $6^1/_2$" x $6^1/_2$". Repeat to cut 20 **B**, 20 **C**, and 20 **D** squares.

From binding fabric:
- Cut 6 binding strips $2^1/_2$" x 40".

MAKING THE QUILT TOP

*Follow **Piecing**, page 10, and **Pressing**, page 12, to make the Quilt Top. Use a 1/4" seam allowance for all sewing.*

1. Referring to your **Quilt Top Layout**, arrange your squares into Rows on a table or on the floor.
2. To make Row 1, work from left to right across the row, to sew a **C** square to a **D** square as shown in **Fig. 1**. Press the seam allowances toward the **D** square.

Fig. 1

3. Continue adding one square at a time, pressing the seam allowances in the same direction after each addition, until Row 1 is finished. Make 2 Row 1's.

4. Pressing the seam allowances of odd numbered rows in one direction and even numbered rows in the opposite direction, repeat Steps 2 and 3 to make 2 of each Row 2, Row 3, and Row 4. Make 1 of Row 5.

5. Matching right sides and raw edges, sew Rows 1 and 2 together as shown in (**Fig. 2**). Continue adding one row at a time to complete the **Quilt Top**.

Fig. 2

TYING AND FINISHING

*Tying is a type of quilting. Quilts can be tied with yarn, embroidery floss, pearl cotton, or ribbon. Refer to the X's on the **Quilt Top Diagram** for placement when tying your quilt top.*

1. Follow **Quilting**, page 12, to mark your quilt top, piece your backing (trim the prepared backing to 62" x 62"), layer, and then pin-baste your quilt sandwich.

2. Thread a large crewel needle with 2 strands of yarn (about 18" long). Do **not** tie a knot in the end.

3. Beginning at placement mark closest to the center and leaving about an 8" "tail" of yarn showing on the Quilt Top, take a small stitch that goes through all three layers of the quilt and back up to the top. Leaving another 8" tail, cut the yarn (**Fig. 3**).

Fig. 3

4. Tie the two tails into a square knot (**Fig. 4**). Trim the tails to about 1" long.

Fig. 4

5. Re-threading your needle as needed, repeat Steps 3 and 4 to make a tie at each placement mark on the **Quilt Top Diagram**. Remove the safety pins.

6. Follow **Finishing**, page 15 , to add a hanging sleeve, bind, and label your quilt.

Quilt Top Diagram

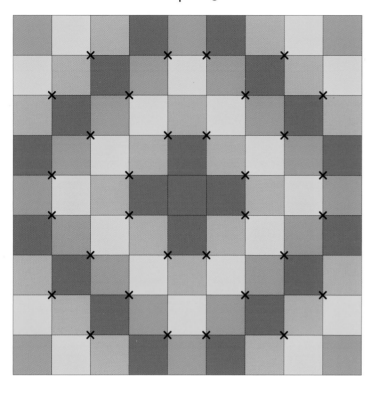

Now you know how to plan and design a Trip Around the World quilt! Maybe you would like to make another one using a different color combination to use as a gift for a special person!

Quilt Top Layout

Row									
1	D	C	B	A	D	A	B	C	D
2	C	B	A	D	C	D	A	B	C
3	B	A	D	C	B	C	D	A	B
4	A	D	C	B	A	B	C	D	A
5	D	C	B	A	A	A	B	C	D
4	A	D	C	B	A	B	C	D	A
3	B	A	D	C	B	C	D	A	B
2	C	B	A	D	C	D	A	B	C
1	D	C	B	A	D	A	B	C	D

Block
A B C & D

LESSON 7

PINWHEEL THROW

Whether you want a cozy throw to snuggle under or colorful wall hanging for your room, this cheerful quilt is sure to brighten your day! Learn how to make Triangle-Squares, use the Triangle-Squares to make Pinwheel Blocks, add borders, layer a quilt "sandwich", and hand quilt.

Finished Quilt Size:
47" x 55" (119 cm x 140 cm)

Finished Block Size:
8" x 8" (20 cm x 20 cm)

FABRIC REQUIREMENTS

*Refer to **What You Need**, page 4, and **Fabrics**, page 5, to help you select your supplies and prepare your fabrics. Yardage amounts are based on using 43/44" (109/112 cm) wide fabric.*

$1^3/_4$ yds (1.6 m) of yellow tone-on-tone print
$^5/_8$ yd (57 cm) of blue print
2 yds (1.8 m) of red floral
$3^1/_2$ yds (3.2 m) of backing fabric

You will also need:
15 red $^3/_4$" (19 mm) diameter buttons
Yellow embroidery floss
$1^1/_2$" (38 mm) long safety pins
51" x 59" (130 cm x 150 cm) rectangle of batting

CUTTING OUT THE PIECES

*If using scissors to cut fabric, follow **Scissor Cutting**, page 6, to cut large pieces A & D-F and to use pattern B & C, page 51. If using a rotary cutter to cut fabrics, follow **Rotary Cutting**, page 8, to cut pieces A-F*

From yellow tone-on-tone print:

- If **scissor cutting**, cut 15 setting squares $8^1/_2$" x $8^1/_2$" (**A**) and 30 squares (**B**). If **rotary cutting**, cut 4 strips $8^1/_2$" wide and 4 strips $4^7/_8$" wide. From the $8^1/_2$" wide strips, cut 15 setting squares $8^1/_2$" x $8^1/_2$" (**A**). From the $4^7/_8$" wide strips, cut 30 squares $4^7/_8$" x $4^7/_8$" (**B**).

From blue print:

- If **scissor cutting**, cut 30 squares (**C**). If **rotary cutting**, cut 4 strips $4^7/_8$" wide. From these strips, cut 30 squares $4^7/_8$" x $4^7/_8$" (**C**).

From red floral:

- Cut 6 crosswise binding strips $2^1/_2$" x 40" (**F**).
- Cut 2 lengthwise side borders $3^1/_2$" x $50^1/_2$" (**D**).
- Cut 2 lengthwise top and bottom borders $3^1/_2$" x $48^1/_2$" (**E**).

MAKING THE PINWHEEL BLOCKS

*Follow **Piecing**, page 10, and **Pressing**, page 12, to make the Quilt Top. Use a $^1/_4$" seam allowance for all sewing.*

1. Use a fabric marking pencil to draw a diagonal line (corner to corner) on the wrong side of each **B** square. Draw stitching lines, $^1/_4$" on either side of the center line (**Fig. 1**). With right sides together, place 1 **B** square on top of 1 **C** square. Sew squares together on stitching lines (**Fig. 2**).

Fig. 1

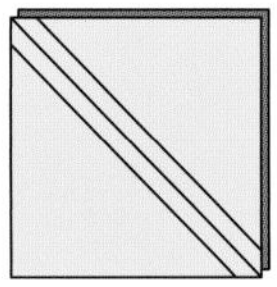

Fig. 2

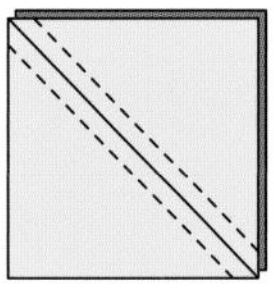

2. Cut apart on the center line as shown in **Fig. 3**. Open up each half and press to make 2 **Triangle-Squares**. Make 60 Triangle-Squares.

Fig. 3

Triangle-Squares (make 60)

3. Lay out 4 Triangle-Squares, as shown in **Pinwheel Block Diagram**, to form a pinwheel. Sew the top 2 Triangle-Squares together, and then sew the bottom 2 Triangle-Squares together (**Fig. 4**). Sew the top and bottom sections together to make a **Pinwheel Block**. Make 15 Pinwheel Blocks.

Fig. 4

Pinwheel Block (make 15)

MAKING THE QUILT TOP CENTER

*Refer to the **Quilt Top Diagram**, page 50, to assemble the quilt top center.*

1. Sew 3 **A** squares and 2 Pinwheel Blocks together to make **Row 1**. Make 3 Row 1's.

Row 1 (make 3)

2. Sew 2 **A** squares and 3 Pinwheel Blocks together to make **Row 2**. Make 3 Row 2's.

Row 2 (make 3)

3. Starting with a Row 1 and alternating Row 1's and Row 2's, sew the Rows together to complete the **Quilt Top Center**.

DID YOU KNOW?

The Aids Memorial Quilt is made up of approximately 46,000 individual 3' x 6' panels. Each panel was made in memory of a person (or persons) who has died from Aids. If all the panels were laid end to end it would be 51.5 miles long.

48

ADDING THE BORDERS

The borders are cut longer than needed to allow for differences in sewing. Following the steps below, measure and trim the borders to the correct length before sewing them to your Quilt Top Center.

1. Measure the **length** through the middle of the Quilt Top Center and trim the side borders **D** to this measurement (**Fig. 5**).

Fig. 5

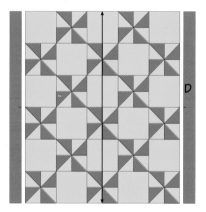

2. Mark the center of each edge of the Quilt Top Center. Mark the center of each side border.

3. With right sides together, match and pin the side borders to the Quilt Top Center at the center marks and corners, easing in any extra length. Sew the side borders to the Quilt Top Center.

4. Measure the **width** through the middle of the Quilt Top Center, including the side borders and trim the top and bottom borders **E** to this measurement. Mark the center of each top and bottom border (**Fig. 6**).

Fig. 6

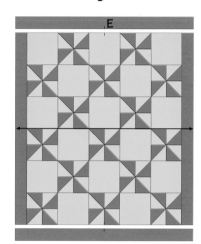

5. With right sides together, match and pin the top and bottom borders to the Quilt Top Center at the center marks and corners, easing in any extra length. Sew the top and bottom borders to the Quilt Top Center.

QUILTING AND FINISHING

1. Follow **Quilting**, page 12, to mark your quilt top, piece your backing (trim the prepared backing to 51" x 59"), layer, and then pin-baste your quilt sandwich.

2. Referring to the **Quilt Top Diagram**, page 50, quilt a diamond in each setting square using 2 strands of yellow embroidery floss.

3. Going through all 3 layers, sew a button to the center of each Pinwheel Block.

4. Follow **Finishing**, page 15, to add a hanging sleeve, bind using binding strips **F**, and label your quilt.

Quilt Top Diagram

Congratulations,
your quilt is finished!
You can enjoy snuggling
under your new creation
while you plan your
next project!

Block
B & C

METRIC CONVERSION CHART

Inches x 2.54 = centimeters (cm)	Yards x .9144 = meters (m)
Inches x 25.4 = millimeters (mm)	Yards x 91.44 = centimeters (cm)
Inches x .0254 = meters (m)	Centimeters x .3937 = inches (")
	Meters x 1.0936 = yards (yd)

Standard Equivalents

1/8"	3.2 mm	0.32 cm	1/8 yard	11.43 cm	0.11 m
1/4"	6.35 mm	0.635 cm	1/4 yard	22.86 cm	0.23 m
3/8"	9.5 mm	0.95 cm	3/8 yard	34.29 cm	0.34 m
1/2"	12.7 mm	1.27 cm	1/2 yard	45.72 cm	0.46 m
5/8"	15.9 mm	1.59 cm	5/8 yard	57.15 cm	0.57 m
3/4"	19.1 mm	1.91 cm	3/4 yard	68.58 cm	0.69 m
7/8"	22.2 mm	2.22 cm	7/8 yard	80 cm	0.8 m
1"	25.4 mm	2.54 cm	1 yard	91.44 cm	0.91 m

LOOKING AHEAD!

Now that you have learned all the quilting basics, why not mix and match some techniques for your next projects? For example, you could:

- Tie a Pinwheel Quilt instead of using hand quilting.
- Hand quilt a Trip Around the World Quilt instead of tying.
- Appliqué the heart from the Sewing Caddy onto a Tote Bag.
- Use a few photo transfer blocks in the place of a few plain blocks in a Trip Around the World Quilt.
- Make a larger quilt by adding more blocks (remember, you will also need to increase the size of borders, batting, backing, and bindings to fit your quilt top).

We have made every effort to ensure that these instructions are accurate and complete. We cannot, however, be responsible for human error, typographical mistakes, or variations in individual work.

Production Team: Technical Editor – Lisa Lancaster; Editorial and Technical Writer – Jean Lewis; Production Artist – Stephanie Hamling; Photography Stylist – Sondra Daniels

ISBN 1-57486-635-4

 PRINTED WITH SOY INK

 Made in U.S.A.